Keep your ~~Marriage~~ Safe

SAFE HOUSE

A PRACTICAL GUIDE TO SAFE GUARD YOUR HEART AND YOUR MARRIAGE FROM THE ENEMY

Cheryl Polote-Williamson

Cheryl Polote-Williamson

Table of Contents

Acknowledgments

First, I want to give honor and praise to God who is my rock, my salvation, my fortress and my shield. You have hidden me beneath your wing. I have found shelter and refuge under your shadow. You have protected me, comforted me, and cared for me. You have kept me. You breathed new life into me when I thought all hope was gone. For that, I am eternally grateful.

To my husband Russell M. Williamson, I thank you. When I found it impossible to stand on my own, you stood with me. Truly we have bared one another's burdens. We have held one another together through trying times and together have proclaimed the goodness and faithfulness of God. You have given me so many reasons to rejoice. I love you.

To my amazing children, Russ Jr., Lauren, and Courtney, and to my dear grandbaby Leah, you all are truly a prize from God. I look at you and am constantly encouraged to be the best me possible. You are my heart's joy. You are my why. I love you with everything in me.

To my parents, Benjamin and Gretta Polote Sr., I honor you always. Your unconditional love never fails. You have taught me so much. Your words, lessons, and encouragement have carried me through many dark hours into brighter days. I thank you and I love you.

To my siblings and the rest of my family, immediate and extended, what a joy it is to be surrounded by so much love and know that people genuinely care. Thank you for your love, encouragement, and support. You are very much appreciated.

To the truest friends a person can have. You know who you are. I LOVE YOU! Thank you for praying for me, lifting me, loving me, believing in me, and supporting me. You have redefined the meaning of friendship for me and I could not be more thankful.

Special thank you to Vladimire Calixte, Alexandria L. Barlowe, the Polote, Williamson, and Green families and the beautiful ladies of the award-winning Blessings, Business, and Collaborations Facebook Group. I love you all!

Foreword

We live in a society where the perception or definition of marriage has become all but lost amongst innumerable personal interpretations. Therefore, there is a great need to engage in a deeper discussion. Amid pervasive confusion regarding the understanding of marriage, it is easy to lose sight of what we believe. The Bible contains many references to God's purpose for marriage as it is one of the most central themes in scripture. For example:

Genesis 2:24: "Therefore a man shall leave his father and his mother and hold fast to his wife, and they shall become one flesh."

Ecclesiastes 4:9: "Two are better than one, because they have a good return for their labor: If either of them falls down, one can help the other up. But pity anyone who falls and has no one to help them up. Also, if two lie down together, they will keep warm. But how can one keep warm alone?"

Isaiah 54:5: "For your Maker is your husband, the LORD of hosts is his name; and the Holy One of Israel is your Redeemer, the God of the whole earth he is called."

Malachi 2:14-15: "But you say, 'Why does he not?' Because the LORD was witness between you and the wife of your youth, to whom you have been faithless, though she is your companion and your wife by covenant."

Mark 10:9: "Therefore what God has joined together, let no one separate.

Ephesians 5:25-33: "Husbands, love your wives, as Christ loved the church and gave himself up for her, that he might sanctify her, having cleansed her by the washing of water with the word, so that he might present the church to himself in splendor, without spot or wrinkle or any such thing, that she might be holy and without blemish. In the same way husbands, should love their wives as their own bodies. He who loves his wife loves himself. For no one ever hated his own flesh, but nourishes and cherishes it, just as Christ does the church."

Colossians 3:14: "And over all these virtues put on love, which binds them all together in perfect unity."

The aforementioned scriptures represent a very close connection between marriage and God. Why? Because marriage is a covenant! A covenant celebrated between a man and a woman, becoming one flesh, in the marriage bed. In turn, marriage also emphasizes God's sacred covenant with us, His people. God intended marriage to meet our need for companionship, partnership, intimacy and the ability to pursue Him together. Thus, providing an example of our relationship with God.

"Marriage is two people sharing life, committed to the highest dreams of what it means to give, to love and be loved. Meant to shine, make you shiver and challenge you to reach your best as a human being. The crucible of unique passion and aliveness between two soul-mates where individuality shines, honoring both lovers who revel in the uniqueness of their mate."   -   Doug and Leslie Gustafson

So often we see the opposite. What happens when the sanctity and cherished bonds of marriage are broken, as a result of betrayal and infidelity? How can we move forward past the pain to heal together? Albeit a difficult road, it is necessary to take these steps to restore and create hope:

1. Go back to the foundation, which is God. Thus, ensuring greater emotional intimacy.

2. Be willing to share personal emotional responsibility. Hence, the need to ask some critical questions such as "what role do I play in what we are experiencing?"

3. Create a mutual agreement to start anew through forgiveness.

As a Christian first and couples' therapist second, I wholeheartedly believe that healthy marriages are not accidental. A safeguarded marriage is the result of fervent and consistent prayer, forgiveness, affection, commitment, honesty, mutual trust and respect. Love can grow again!

In this day and age, we have home security systems, car alarms, and computer virus spyware. Additionally, we take vitamins and eat the right foods to bolster our immune systems. We put on masks and hazardous material suits to protect ourselves from toxins. We wear sunscreen for protection. However, at times, we are lax about protecting our marriage. What are you doing to arm and protect your marriage? What systems have you put in place to safeguard your union? If the answer to these questions is nothing, Safe House will help change that.

Vladimire Calixte MA, CRC, LMHC

Couples Therapist

New York, NY

www.LifeRebuilding.net

Preface

A safe house is a secret location that provides sanctuary to those who may be in danger. **Psalm 27:5 "For in the day of trouble, he will conceal me in his tabernacle; in the secret place of His tent He will hide me, He will lift me up on a rock."**

When I decided to write this book, I had two main purposes in mind. One was to equip readers with the wisdom of God which will help to discern threats that may be lurking and attempting to destroy their marriage. When a marriage is headed for trouble, there are always warning signs. Every single time. If you are not spiritually in tune with God, your mate and those who are around you, it could be very easy to overlook or dismiss those signs. Unfortunately, missing warning signs is a critical mistake that is made too often; the consequences can be far reaching and long lasting. However, this book will provide you with some sure-fire ways to spot those red flags and what to do once you have spotted them.

My second and most important purpose for writing this book is to encourage you that there is hope and a chance for life, love and marriage after betrayal. **Ecclesiastes 9:4** says **"but for him who is joined to all the living there is hope, for a living dog is better than a dead lion."** In summary, this tells us that where there is life there is hope. You may find yourself or your marriage in a broken place but please know that you are not alone. I am here to tell you that although you may be broken, you are not dead. As long as there is breath in your body, there is hope for your situation! God has allowed you to be in this place of your life for a time but certainly not forever.

Ecclesiastes 3:1 "To everything there is a season, a time for every purpose under heaven."

In spite of what you may be going through, you must know and be confident in the fact that He has graced you for this time in your life. He has allowed you to have painful experiences to strengthen and better you. He is not picking on you and he has not forgotten you. He is loading up your tool belt. Your painful experiences are bricks in the interior walls of your Safe House.

Jeremiah 29:11 "For I know the thoughts that I think toward you, says the Lord, thoughts of peace and not of evil, to give you a future and a hope."

I want to minister to you by telling you the story of a couple I know. Kenneth and Lacey were the type of couple you see in sappy romance movies. They were sickeningly head over heels for each other. I'm talking major public displays of affection, finishing each other's sentences, rarely arguing and countless other acts of overwhelming and all-consuming love. These two were annoyingly perfect for each other. I am not telling you Kenneth and Lacey's story just for fun or because it is a good one. I am telling you their story because you need to hear it. Consider the very fact that you picked up this book a divine appointment.

Before you continue reading, I ask that you do a few things. Please grab your Bible and something to write with. Please use the lined pages of this book to write down your feelings and thoughts as you read. I challenge you to be completely honest and do not hold back. Consider this divine appointment just that, an appointment. Try to set a specific time to read this book each day. Safe House would be the perfect addition to time in your prayer closet. This appointment will change your life, if you let it. More importantly, it will equip you with the necessary tools to weather storms and emerge victorious from the battles within your marriage.

Throughout this book, you will find prayers and scriptures to refer to. Open your heart and allow God to speak through each prayer and scripture. You will also find reflection questions that will require you to remember and analyze certain situations and to think critically about certain people in your life. These questions are designed to help you to apply the lessons that can be learned from Kenneth and Lacey's story. They are also designed to provide you with wisdom on how to spot warning signs and how to respond to them. This is your how-to, instruction manual, "for dummies" guide on how to guard your marriage from the enemy. This will teach you how to turn your heart and home into a Safe House, where the enemy certainly is not welcome and not able to intrude.

Dear Heavenly Father,

Thank you for this divine appointment. Thank you for loving me enough to direct me to this guide. Thank you for caring about me enough to provide me with encouragement to weather the storms of love and marriage. God, I ask that you infuse my mind and spirit with wisdom. Meet me here God. Minister to me through this story and let it strengthen me to pass the tests that I am facing in my marriage. I ask that you help me to see my spouse through your eyes, in spite of anything that we have experienced or may be currently experiencing. Enrich our union and bless it to forever glorify your name. I invite your word into my home, my mind, body and spirit as I read this book. Thank you for your providing me with the tools that I need to build my Safe House. In your name, I pray, amen.

Proverbs 1:5 (NKJV)

"A wise man will increase learning, and a man of understanding will attain wise counsel."

Chapter 1: Meet Kenneth and Lacey

The Romance

Proverbs 5:18 "May your fountain be blessed and may you rejoice in the wife of thy youth."

Proverbs 18:22 "He who finds a wife finds a good thing and obtains favor from the Lord."

Lacey and Kenneth met and married in the early 1990's. When they met, Kenneth was a respected officer in the Air Force. Kenneth was born and raised in Harlem, New York. He was raised by a single mother who struggled to make ends meet. With Kenneth and a younger brother to feed on very little income, times were tough for his mother. From a very early age, Kenneth was determined to overcome the perils of poverty and make a successful life for himself. Through perseverance, hard work, and dedication he did just that.

Lacey was an up and coming entrepreneur. She was born in Atlanta, Georgia in what most would call the "upper crust" of society. Unlike Kenneth, Lacey was a stranger to financial struggle. Her father had become independently wealthy when he built his private law firm. She had everything she wanted and needed. Her life was a series of tennis lessons, Jack and Jill meetings and cotillions. Although her family was of means, they taught her the importance of hard work and humility as a child.

Just like in the romance novels, Kenneth and Lacey fell in love via love letters during Kenneth's eight-month deployment in the Persian Gulf. After retiring from the military, Kenneth would go on to work for a highly profitable pharmaceutical company. Throughout the years, Kenneth's career took their family on many amazing adventures that often-included relocation. Although Lacey was grateful for the opportunities that

Kenneth's work afforded them, the constant relocation began to take its toll on their family. Lacey had to deal with the stress of packing up their belongings, uprooting the children, enrolling them in new schools, etc. It was Lacey's faith in God and fervent prayer life that kept her at peace amidst the constant changes during that period of their life. On the eve of their 24th anniversary, Lacey found herself reminiscing about the early days of her marriage. One of her fondest memories of their life together was their wedding day.

Simply put, she was in heaven. Her state of mind was nothing less than pure bliss. She was completely and totally enraptured. She could not believe that her dream had finally come true. She had never loved anyone as much as she loved Kenneth. She knew that their love would last forever and was ready to sail off into the sunset with her Prince Charming. She put on her diamond chandelier earrings, the Tiffany tennis bracelet he bought her for their six-month anniversary, and did one final check of her hair and makeup before walking out of the bridal chamber and into the main sanctuary.

As her soft brown eyes met his, she could see him melt as a tear leaked slowly down his cheek. She dreamt of this day since she was a young girl and now here she was preparing to walk down the aisle to marry her best friend and the love of her life; a man who was literally moved to tears at the sight of her in her beautiful white gown. She finally reached him after what seemed like an hour-long march down that aisle. His tears were still flowing as he bit his lip doing his best to maintain his composure.

"You look so beautiful." He managed to utter, the lump in his throat muddling his otherwise velvety voice.

By this time, she was crying too.

"Thank God for waterproof mascara." She thought to herself.

She gazed at him lovingly as he lifted her veil and gently wiped a tear from her eye. She wanted to kiss him right then and there.

"Dearly beloved, we are gathered here today...." The preacher began.

"Are you nervous yet?" He whispered to his bride as the preacher read the familiar words that preceded the vows at weddings.

"Nope. Not even a little bit." She replied.

"I have been waiting for this day for as long as I can remember." She added.

"I have too, Lacey. I have too." He responded.

It's disgustingly cliché but no one sees or even imagines what lies ahead on their wedding day. Majority of couples are completely submerged in the thickness of their love for one another. On that day, neither the bride or the groom imagine that someone they trust could shake the foundation of their marriage to its core. They never entertain the notion that something that may appear to be the end of their marriage could be the very thing that strengthens it. Perhaps none of these things cross their minds because they are blinded by the perfectly sewn lace on the custom wedding gown, the meticulously tailored tux, or the gorgeous cake that nearly touches the sky.

Oh, and who could forget the pictures? Those breathtaking pictures. No house is a home without the ever so stunning wedding photos. Although they are lovely and one of the most celebrated parts of a wedding day, marriage is not just about the photos. Those people in the photos are real flawed human beings. Human beings that can change, grow apart and even be corrupted by forces that are not of this world.

What if I told you that in spite of the trials and tribulations you may face, God can make your life and your marriage just as beautiful as those photos? What if I told you that God would allow you and your spouse to endure some of your darkest days so that you could bind together and walk in the sunlight of His purpose for your marriage? What if I also told you that he wants you be discerning about people and situations that may come against your marriage?

Reflection: Take a moment to think back to your own wedding day. If possible, pull out your wedding photos or watch your wedding video. Think back to how you felt that day. Did you have a big ceremony? A small intimate ceremony with only your closest friends and family? How did you feel about your spouse that day? What were your hopes and dreams for your future together?

Dear Heavenly Father,

Please forgive me for my sins. Please create in me a clean heart and renew my commitment to my marriage and my spouse. Help us to look at each other the same way we did on the day that we exchanged vows. God, I ask that you strengthen our bond and help us to turn to you to fight the enemy that seeks to destroy our marriage. I consider these things done, father.

In your name, I pray, amen.

Revelation 21:5 "Then he who sat on the throne said, "behold, I make all things new." And he said to me, "Write, for these words are true and faithful."

Psalm 51:10 "Create in me a clean heart, O God. Renew a loyal spirit within me."

The Kids

Psalm 127: 3 "Behold, children are a heritage from the Lord, the fruit of the womb is a reward."

When Kenneth and Lacey first married, Kenneth was eager to start a family right away. Lacey was happy to oblige.

"Well?! What does it say Lacey?!" Kenneth shouted impatiently from the other side of the bathroom door.

"It hasn't been five minutes yet, Kenny." Lacey replied.

She laughed to herself as she could hear the anticipation in her husband's voice. His excitement nearly overshadowed her anxiety as she stared nervously at the little piece of plastic that could possibly deliver life changing news in the next four and a half minutes. Would she see one pink line or two?

"Let's see, one line means not pregnant and two lines mean pregnant." Lacey said still staring at the pregnancy test.

"Gosh this is taking forever." She thought to herself.

"Laaaaace! Anything yet?!" Kenneth shouted again.

"No honey, you asked just thirty seconds ago. It takes five minutes to get the results!" Lacey responded again laughing to herself.

She thought Kenneth's nervousness was cute, endearing actually. She felt fortunate to have a man who was this excited about starting a family. After what seemed like an eternity, the pregnancy test results finally appeared in that two-inch window. Lacey saw two pink lines.

Kenneth Junior or KJ as they called him was born in August of 1991, just before Kenneth and Lacey's first anniversary. It was love at first sight when they finally met their bundle of joy after nine long months of anticipation.

"He looks just like my baby pictures," Kenneth said tearfully as he held his son for the first time.

"He does have your nose," Lacey added.

Lacey felt an immediate connection to motherhood. She fell naturally into the role the minute they brought KJ Home from the hospital. Their sweet baby boy brought more joy to their life than they knew was humanly possible. With every laugh, cry and cuddle, Kenneth and Lacey fell more in love with KJ and of course, more in love with each other. Lacey was so grateful that she was able to be present for all of those special firsts in a baby's life. Kenneth's hectic work schedule kept him at work and on the road majority of the time. Before they knew it, Kenneth and Lacey were planning to celebrate KJ's third birthday.

"Oh my goodness, honey do you remember this picture?" Lacey asked as she pulled a picture out of the photo album and walked over to show it to Kenneth.

She was gathering photos of KJ to have on display at his party which was set to take place that afternoon. Lacey worked on the party details and decorations as Kenneth sat at his desk, working from home as he always did.

"Wow, I do remember babe. I remember like it was yesterday." Kenneth replied as he took the photo from Lacey.

"How was this already three years ago?" He asked as he stared at the photo of his wife holding KJ in the hospital as they were getting ready to bring him home.

"I was so mad at you because you forgot to bring the outfit that I wanted to take him home in. Do you remember honey?" Lacey asked as she remembered her irritation that day. It was funny now but that day she was livid.

"Yes, I remember." Kenneth responded. He was not laughing at all. In fact, he looked as if he might cry.

"Kenny baby what is wrong?" Lacey asked touching his arm.

"I feel like time is going by so fast, you know? I mean, it's like yesterday we were bringing him home from the hospital. Now he is turning three. I remember every detail of the day you had him so vividly. I hate that I have had to miss so much of these first few years." Kenneth explained.

"The time has definitely flown by honey. I can't believe it either. You have missed a lot. Of course, it hurts and KJ is too young to understand that daddy has to work to provide for us. I guess I have gotten used to that being how our life works these days. Before you know it, he is going to be starting Kindergarten. You just remember, that job will always be there but your baby boy won't always be a baby." Lacey said.

"I know you are right honey. I'm going to do better at spending quality time with both of you. Starting today. Give me some of this birthday stuff you're playing with. What can I do to help?" Kenneth asked grabbing a balloon off of the table.

"Blowing up that balloon is a great start. I've got a couple dozens of them here, you can get to those after you finish that one!" Lacey replied.

She picked up a balloon to blow up herself but was stopped abruptly by a sudden feeling of nausea. She tried to shrug it off but with each passing second, she could feel her stomach churning.

"Kenny honey, I don't feel so good." She said staggering towards the bathroom.

Unfortunately, her stomach did not care about letting her make it to the bathroom before it decided to empty itself on to their kitchen floor. As she stood slumped over the counter, she knew this could only mean one thing.

"Kennyyyyyy!" She yelled.

"Yeah babe?" He replied from the living room where he was working on blowing up the balloons.

"You're gonna have to blow up all of those balloons by yourself." Lacey stammered, clutching her stomach and still hanging on to the counter."

"Why?" Kenneth asked walking into the kitchen.

"Oh goodness, baby what is that smell? Wait, did you just...?" Kenneth asked with a puzzled look on his face.

"Yep." Lacey interrupted.

"Wait, are you...?" Kenneth said pointing at her stomach.

"Yep." Lacey interrupted again.

Kenneth hopped over the puddle and swept Lacey over off her feet.

"I am so happy woman! We're having another one!" Kenny shouted as squeezed Lacey tight.

Seven months later Lacey and Kenneth welcomed their second child.

"You don't like Lillian?" Lacey asked sadly as she held their newborn.

"No, babe. I don't like Lillian." Kenneth replied.

"I like Ashley! Ashley! Ashley! Ashley!" KJ shouted jumping up and down excitedly.

"Okay okay! KJ, we hear you little man." Kenneth said laughing.

"Guess we don't have a choice, do we?" Lacey said laughing as well.

"It sounds like we don't. We will call her Ashley." Kenneth added.

Lacey and Kenneth were overjoyed with their recently expanded family. They could not believe how God had blessed them with two wonderful children. It was like each child added a new layer of love to their home. They felt as if life could not get any sweeter. They realized they were wrong just three years later. Life did get sweeter when they welcomed another baby girl. They decided to name her Kelsey. Once again they found themselves in the hospital holding their newborn.

"Aw man! Another one?" KJ griped.

"Yes honey, another one." Lacey replied as she motioned he and Ashley over to see their baby sister.

"She looks weird." KJ said snarkily.

"Don't say that about your sister." Kenneth lectured as he thumped KJ on his hand.

"Ouch dad!" KJ shouted back.

"I wanted a brother! Not another sister!" KJ shouted folding his arms and stomping his feet in disappointment.

"Play! I want play!" Ashley babbled as she jumped out of her chair and into the middle of the hospital room. She bumped into a tray and knocked over a glass of water. She stood there looking scared.

"I sorry!" She stammered.

"Kenneth, come get your kids." Lacey said laughing.

"These are *your* kids." He replied jokingly.

The Careers

Proverbs 10:4 (NIV) "Lazy hands make for poverty but diligent hands bring wealth."

"Honey have you seen my briefcase?!" Kenneth shouted frantically as he raced down the stairs.

"Look in the office!" Lacey yelled from their bedroom upstairs.

"KJ! Go help your sister find something to wear." Lacey yelled down the hall.

"Mommmmm do I have to?!" He moaned in protest.

"Yes, son you have to!" Lacey shot back.

Mornings at their household were nothing less than chaotic. Someone was always crying. Someone was always sleep when should have been in the shower. Someone was always too quiet, which was never a good sign with a ten-year-old, a six-year-old and a three-year-old. Silence meant something mischievous was happening. Kenneth was always looking for something. His shoes, his briefcase, or his cuff links, it was always something.

"Can we have a peaceful morning just once?" Lacey asked herself as she wiped Ashley's face with a wet washcloth.

She quickly pulled her daughter's soft curls up into pigtails and then rounded up the gang to drop KJ and Ashley off at school.

"Mommy, I go to school?" Kelsey shouted from the backseat.

"Not yet baby girl. You get to hang out with mommy all day. Then when you are a big girl, you go to school." Lacey explained.

"I big girl now mommy! I go to school!" Kelsey exclaimed.

"Not yet, baby girl." Lacey responding laughing.

KJ and Ashley were in the back seat fighting over something per usual.

"That's enough you two." Lacey snapped shooting them a serious look through the rearview mirror.

She was relieved when they finally pulled up to drop off at the school.

"Alright loves, everyone behaves today. Have a great day. I love you." Lacey said unlocking the back door to let them out.

"Love you too ma." They responded in unison lackadaisically.

She headed back home, her youngest in tow.

For majority of their marriage, Lacey had put her goals and desires on the back burner to raise the children and support Kenneth as he furthered his career. Lacey had been a stay at home mother for the past ten years. Although she loved being at home with her children, she was eager for a career of her own. Now that their oldest two children were in school, Lacey had more flexibility in her schedule. She was able to manage just one small child running around as opposed to three. Lacey spent three years crafting her brand as a successful motivational speaker and author. She had become an expert at juggling parent teacher conferences and conference calls with investors. She mastered the art of scheduling business meetings around soccer practices, recitals and birthday parties.

One of the best things about Kenneth and Lacey was that they prided themselves on their philanthropic efforts. Through these efforts, they garnered a great deal of respect amongst their circle of friends and within their community. They had it all. A beautiful home, luxury cars, enviable wardrobes and three wonderful children who excelled in school. From the outside looking in, they were living the dream.

Journal Page

_____

_____

_____

_____

_____

_____

_____

_____

_____

Chapter 2: Matthew 10:16

"Behold, I send you out as sheep in the midst of wolves. Therefore, be wise as serpents and gentle as doves."

As aforementioned, Kenneth's job often required relocation. Over a span of ten years, their family moved a total of eight times. Eventually, their family landed in Dallas, Texas. With Kenneth's executive role at his company and Lacey's budding business, black tie affairs became a regular part of their schedule. It seemed like they were off to another gala every other night. At times, Lacey felt like she spent her entire life getting ready for a formal event. One thing that always frustrated Lacey was having to find a new hair stylist whenever they relocated. It may seem like a minor thing but it was not. Not when you have formal events several times per month. These things required a team! That team included a hair stylist and makeup artist.

"Kenneth, I have no idea who is going to fix this mess for the auction on Thursday." Lacey said pointing at her hair.

"You may just have to tell them we can't go. Tell them I'm not feeling well or something." She added.

"Baby, can't you fix your hair yourself?" Kenneth uttered.

Lacey shot him a dirty look.

"No, Kenneth I cannot do my own hair. Not for an event." She rebutted.

"Lace how about this? There is a girl who does hair at my barber shop. I've seen some of the ladies she's worked on and their hair looked nice when she finished. It looks like she does decent work." Kenneth answered.

"I don't know Kenneth. Trying a new hair stylist is always risky." Lacey responded.

"Look, baby. Here's the number. Just give her a call and try her out. If you don't like what she does with your hair, we won't go to the gala on Thursday. Is that a deal?" Kenneth asked trying to cheer her up.

"Ok. I think I can handle that. I'll give her a call now." Lacey replied taking the business card from him.

Years later, Lacey would regret making that call.

Her name was Shawndra. Thankfully, she did a great job on Lacey's hair that night and they hit it off immediately. Before long, Lacey was visiting her weekly for hair appointments. They became closer with each appointment and eventually Shawndra became like part of the family. Lacey and Shawndra confided in each other, helped each other and formed what seemed to be a lifelong bond. Shawndra asked Kenneth and Lacey to be the godparents of her two children.

Lacey invited Shawndra into her exclusive social circle of published authors, motivational speakers, successful doctors, esteemed attorneys and entrepreneurs. This circle also included some of Kenneth's colleagues. Through Lacey, Shawndra's clientele expanded greatly as Lacey referred many people to her on a regular basis. Lacey also provided Shawndra with financial support when she was in need. As a struggling self-employed hair stylist, things were tough for Shawndra at times. However, Lacey was always willing to help when she was in a bind. Over the course their friendship, the two shared many a laugh and some tears as well. One day in particular, the ladies reminisced about a funny incident while having lunch.

"Girl do you remember that time when we were walking home from the play and got chased by that dog?! Shawndra asked sipping her Chai latte.

Lacey did remember that night and she felt like she had never laughed harder. She and Kenneth lived a few blocks away from a popular theatre and Tyler Perry's *I Can Do Bad All By Myself* was playing that night. Lacey and Shawndra decided they would walk from Lacey's house to the play and then have dinner afterwards. Before heading to dinner, they wanted to stop at Lacey's home to change clothes. On the way, they ran into a vicious Chihuahua.

Although he was tiny, this dog was clearly angry and he decided to chase Lacey and Shawndra from the theatre all the way to Lacey's home. They ran screaming down the street for what felt like an hour until they reached Lacey and Kenneth's home. When they finally arrived to safety, they laughed hysterically.

"Oh I remember! How could I ever forget?" Lacey said laughing as she took a bite of her chopped chicken salad.

"Why were we so afraid of a five-pound dog?!" Shawndra asked laughing at the memory of them racing down the street as if they were afraid for their lives.

"Girl I have no idea." Lacey replied also laughing.

"We have had some good times through these years haven't we, girl?" Lacey added.

"We sure have Lacey. We sure have. I'm so glad you are my friend. And you know I love me some Kenneth, girl. How is my handsome man doing?" Shawndra asked jokingly.

"Girl he is fine. Driving me crazy as usual." Lacey responded.

"Well you know I'll take him off of your hands if he gets to be too much trouble!" Shawndra quipped.

They both laughed. On the surface this was a seemingly harmless conversation. Unfortunately, Shawndra's motives were everything but harmless.

"That reminds me, the motor on my garage door burned out yesterday and I was wondering if he could swing by and fix it for me later?" Shawndra asked.

"I will ask him for you when I get home. Is Bernard working late again, girl?" Lacey asked.

"You know how he is Lacey. It's always the job first, me second." Shawndra replied sadly.

Lacey could sense the pain in her eyes. Bernard and Shawndra had been married for five years. Bernard was a kind and gentle man but he and Shawndra had their issues, just like every other married couple. Shawndra seemed to be growing more unhappy with Bernard each day. She was normally a bubbly person with high energy but when the subject of her marriage came up, her chipper spirit deflated like a balloon that had been suddenly popped.

When the scripture Matthew 10:16 says to be wise as a serpent and gentle as a dove, God is commanding us to use wisdom and be discerning in situations that could potentially harm us. Throughout their friendship, Lacey noticed things about Shawndra that made her uncomfortable. They were minor things so Lacey usually shrugged them off but they did catch her attention. For example, Shawndra always talked about how she could never keep female friends because they always turned on her. She explained that they turned on her because they were jealous of her looks and the attention she got from men.

Does this sound like any of the women in your inner circle?

 Reflection: Take a couple of minutes and think about the last time you had a gut feeling. Think about the situation surrounding this feeling and the state of mind you were in. Now take a few minutes to write some thoughts in the notes section. Go deep here. Be as specific as you can and try to remember precise details. Did you have a physical reaction? For example, goosebumps, hairs standing up on your arms or neck? Maybe a cramp or uncomfortable feeling in the pit of your stomach? Did you feel pressure in your chest or did it suddenly became hard to breathe? Perhaps that awful lump in the back of your throat that almost always precedes tears? Or maybe just an overall feeling of anxiousness, agitation or uneasiness? Those are physical manifestations of your spirit discerning something before your mind has. I'm going to repeat that because you need to let this digest. Those things are physical manifestations of your spirit discerning something before your mind has. If you quickly shrugged off those feelings or ignored them, you may have dismissed some very important warning signs.

Dear Lord,

I thank you for bestowing this blessing of knowledge on me. Please teach me to pay close attention to the signs that you show me. Train me to have a listening ear so that I can actively hear your voice. Open my eyes so that I can clearly see the things that you are trying to reveal to me. Most importantly, show me what to do. Help me to be wise as a serpent and gentle as a dove. Help me to live with a pure heart that is always ready to learn and receive what you have for me.

In your name, I pray, Amen.

Proverbs 1:33 "But whoever listens to me will dwell safely, and will be secure, without fear of evil"

Journal Page

_____

_____

_____

_____

_____

_____

_____

_____

_____

_____

Chapter 3: The Nightmare

"Honey, I'm off to my appointment with Shawndra. What time will Marisol be here?" Lacey yelled from the bottom of the stairs.

"She's on her way now." Kenneth responded.

"Ok perfect. I'll be back in a couple of hours." Lacey said as she walked out the door.

Marisol was their babysitter and Kenneth and Lacey were headed to another gala that evening. Kenneth would stay with the kids until the babysitter arrived so that he could start getting ready.

"I was thinking simple but elegant. Maybe some cascading curls." Lacey instructed.

"You know I got you, Lace! You act like I haven't been doing your hair every week for the past twelve years!" Shawndra retorted.

"I know, I know! You know how I am, girl." Lacey laughed.

"Yes I do! Bossy, overbearing and controlling!" Shawndra snapped jokingly.

"Glad to know you think so highly of me." Lacey shot back.

Reflection: Do you have a friend who is highly critical of you? Does she nitpick things about your personality or your appearance? Does she do it in front of mutual friends or even your husband? Does she laugh or make it seem like she is joking when criticizing you? If you answered yes to any of these, these could be warning signs.

"You know, you should come with me to the Dallas Women's Gala next week." Lacey said changing the subject. That was how she usually responded when someone or something made her uncomfortable.

"Now Lace, you know that is not my scene. I don't want to be around all those uppity people, it makes me nervous." Shawndra explained.

"Girl, you have nothing to be nervous about. You will be with me and Kenneth." Lacey said attempting to change her mind.

"Oh, Kenneth is going with you? I thought you said he was out of town." Shawndra said.

"He is out of town now but he'll be back next week. Just in time for the gala. The gala that you are coming to." Lacey snapped.

"Well if Kenneth is going I guess I can go too." Shawndra said happily.

"Yes! It will be perfect! You should bring Bernard. It will be the perfect double date!" Lacey exclaimed.

"No." Shawndra replied sharply.

"No, what?" Lacey asked.

"I'm not bringing Bernard." Shawndra responded angrily.

"Well why not? I know he works a lot but if you give him a week's notice, can't he figure something out at work? Can he be available for you for just one night?" Lacey asked concerned.

"No. He can't Lace. He's not available. I will be at the gala but I am not bringing Bernard with me. He's not like Kenneth." Shawndra responded.

Reflection: Do you have a female friend that never brings her mate or significant other around? Does she always make excuses about why they aren't around much?

It was obvious that Shawndra was upset but Lacey could not understand why.

"You know Shawndra, for as long as I've known you, he has never been available when you need him. Kenneth does more for you than your own husband. Whenever you need something fixed, you call Kenneth. Does Bernard ever get upset that Kenneth helps out all the time?"

"He's never around to notice so he doesn't know." Shawndra replied coyly.

"You deserve better Shawndra. You know you do. You need to talk to him and tell him how you feel." Lacey pleaded.

"I do talk to him Lace. I talk to him all the time. It doesn't help anything. Not everyone's husband can be like yours." Shawndra replied.

Reflection: Do you have a female friend, colleague or family member who says that they wish their mate was like yours? Are they constantly comparing their husband to yours? These are not things that you should shrug off or dismiss.

Heavenly Father,

I ask that you will reveal the hearts of those who are in my life. Show me who is for me and who is not for me. Give me the discernment to pay attention to the words and actions of those who mean to do me harm and not good. Help and strengthen me to remove those presences in my life. I ask that you separate me from those who are not of you. I believe your word and I consider these things done. In your name, I pray, amen.

Proverbs 2:11-16 "Discretion will preserve you; understanding will keep you, to deliver you from the way of evil, from the man who speaks perverse things, from those who leave the paths of uprightness to walk in the ways of darkness; who rejoice in doing evil and who delight in the perversity of the wicked; whose ways are crooked, and who are devious in their paths; to deliver you from the immoral woman, from the seductress who flatters with her words.

After the Dallas Women's Gala, Kenneth and Lacey went home. Kenneth snored loudly as Lacey tossed and turned for what felt like an hour. When she looked at the clock on their nightstand, it had only been fifteen minutes.

"I wish I could be sound asleep and snoring." Lacey whispered to herself.

She decided that she needed some chamomile tea if she was going to get any sleep that night. Lacey gently pulled back the covers and crept out of their king-sized sleigh bed, careful not to wake Kenneth. She slipped on her satin robe and quietly traipsed down the winding staircase to the kitchen. As she walked past the office, a bright light coming from Kenneth's desk caught her eye. It was hard to miss in the dark. She walked into the office and as she approached his desk, she could see that it was Kenneth's phone.

"Kenneth left his phone down here." She thought to herself.

She grabbed it and continued in to the kitchen. She placed the phone on the island and grabbed her favorite ceramic mug from the cabinet. She was distracted when his phone screen lit up once again. A text message flashed across the screen.

"How could you leave without kissing me goodbye?" It read.

Lacey dropped the mug that she was holding on the kitchen floor. It made a loud clanging noise as the ceramic met the marble and shattered into a dozen pieces. Oddly enough, Lacey didn't hear a thing. Everything fell silent as she stood there frozen, staring at the phone.

"Who sent the text? It was obviously someone that was at the gala that night. Or maybe it was a wrong number. God, please let it be a wrong number." She mumbled to herself.

Thoughts were racing through her mind faster than cars on a Nascar track. Her entire body felt cold. So, cold that by the time she realized that she dropped the mug, she was shivering. Her arms and legs tensed as she heard footsteps on the stairs.

"Babe? Is everything ok? I heard something fall and break, then I realized you weren't in bed. What are you doing?" Kenneth asked as he walked into the kitchen.

"Honey, what's wrong? You look like you've seen a ghost." Kenneth said looking concerned.

"I'm....I'm.... fine." Lacey stammered.

She could barely think clearly enough to get her words out right. Her mouth felt dry and tight as she struggled to speak.

"You left your phone in the office. I....I....I... was going to bring it to you. I came...down to...get some tea...you got a text message Kenneth. Kenneth....who is texting you....at this hour asking for a goodbye kiss?" Lacey asked tearfully.

"What are you talking about Lace?" Kenneth asked.

Lacey picked up his phone with her hands trembling violently and handed it to him.

"You went through my phone?!" Kenneth asked raising his voice.

"No... No..Kenneth. I...I... didn't go through your phone. I told you......you left it in the office....and I was going to bring it to you. I just so happen--"

"You just so happened to snoop through my phone is what it sounds like!" Kenneth snapped.

"No... you are not going to do this. You are not going to make this about me, Kenneth. I'm telling you...I was not going through your phone. I simply saw the text message flash across your screen. It was laying on the counter and I just saw the words flash across your screen." Lacey explained.

By now the shivering had become more intense, violent even. She felt like she had been dropped in a pond that was blanketed by a thick sheet of ice. At this point, Kenneth didn't have to say a word. She already knew. She could tell by his reaction and the tone of his voice. He sounded and acted like a guilty man. It was written all over his face. There was nothing that he could say or do to convince her of his honesty. Why? Because at that moment, honesty and Kenneth did not belong in the same sentence.

"Just tell me her name, Kenneth." Lacey uttered, her lips quivering and voice shaking.

"Lacey, it's not what you think. You've got the wrong idea." Kenneth answered.

"Do not disrespect me any more than you already have by trying to lie your way out of this Kenneth." Lacey sneered through clenched teeth.

"I just want to know her name." She added.

"Lace," he said softly walking towards her with his arms stretched out as if to embrace her.

She smacked his arms away.

"Don't touch me Kenneth! Don't touch me!" Lacey cried.

"You can't even tell me her name, can you?! You coward! Get away from me!" Lacey screamed as she dashed out of the kitchen.

In all of the commotion, she forgot about the shattered mug and stepped on a piece of the fallen ceramic which cut her foot. It began to bleed.

"Lace, your foot!" Kenneth stammered.

"Kenneth I said don't touch me!" She said slapping him across his face.

"Lace you're bleeding!" He pleaded desperately.

She looked down to see the blood flowing from her foot. She didn't feel a thing. She didn't care about the blood at that point. She walked out of the kitchen towards the stairs, ignoring Kenneth's pleas.

"It's Shawndra." Kenneth said.

Lacey stopped dead in her tracks. Suddenly, a surge of pain pulsated from the cut on her foot up to the center of her chest.

"What did you just say?" She asked turning to face Kenneth.

By now he was crying. He dropped his head in shame and fell to his knees.

"Baby, I'm so sorry." He cried.

"What did you say, Kenneth?" Lacey asked again.

"Shawndra." He answered sobbing loudly.

She felt like there were twenty pound bags laying on top of her eyelids as she tried her hardest to open them. Tired and heavy, her eyes struggled to adjust to the bright light that she saw between blinks. Finally, she was able keep them open long enough to realize where she was.

"What's going on? Kenneth?" She mumbled.

Her mouth felt dry and her speech was muddled and sluggish.

"How did I get here?" She thought to herself.

"Kenneth? Are you here?" She asked.

She could hear the beeping of machines, squeaking wheels rushing past the room and the constant clicking and clacking of someone typing rapidly.

"Kenneth??" She shouted.

She heard heavy footsteps coming toward the room. She was so relieved to see Kenneth's tall frame walk through the door. At the same time, she was disgusted as she slowly began to remember what happened before she opened her eyes

"Lace! Baby, I'm so glad you're awake." Kenneth said wrapping his arms around her.

"What happened, Kenneth?" She asked.

"Lacey, you had a heart attack." Kenneth said gently holding her face.

Discovering that Kenneth and Shawndra had been having an affair for the past year was a devastating blow that Lacey had never expected. How could either of them be so cruel? So, conniving? She began to recount every detail that she told Shawndra during her weekly hair appointments over the course of their thirteen-year friendship. She was suddenly flooded with memories of every check she wrote, every client she referred, every event she invited her to; the list went on and on. No wonder she had a heart attack.

Reflection: Have you ever found yourself feeling like Lacey did? Betrayed? Lied to? Cheated on? In **Philippians 4:6-7**, God's word says **"be anxious for nothing, but in everything by prayer and supplication, with thanksgiving, let your requests be made known to God, which surpasses all understanding, will guard your hearts and minds through Christ Jesus."** Easier said than done, right? When something hurtful happens to us, it is normal for us to feel anxious, fearful, angry, or even vengeful. However, God challenges us to take those feelings and turn to him.

Proverbs 3:25-26 and 29 tells us "Do not be afraid of sudden terror, nor of trouble from the wicked when it comes; for the Lord, will be your confidence and will keep your foot from being caught." Do not devise evil against your neighbor, for he dwells by you for safety's sake."

Dear Lord,

Please heal my broken heart. Mend and bind the broken pieces of my marriage. I ask that you turn every tear into triumph and every feeling of sadness into strength. Help me to have a forgiving heart and to work together with my spouse to move past this chapter in our life. Give us the courage to have difficult conversations and face the issues in our marriage head on. Help us to be kind and gracious with one another throughout this process of healing. We thank you in advance for healing and a renewed trust in our home. In your name, I pray, amen.

Journal Page

_____

_____

_____

_____

_____

_____

_____

_____

_____

_____

Chapter 4: Building Your Safe House

You must be wondering what happened to Lacey and Kenneth. Did they get a divorce? Did Kenneth leave Lacey to be with Shawndra? Did Lacey recover from her heart attack? Did Shawndra tell Bernard? How did her affair with Kenneth affect her own marriage? Would you believe me if I told you that Lacey and Kenneth did not get a divorce? What if I told you that Kenneth did not leave Lacey to be with Shawndra? What if I told you that Lacey and Kenneth are still together to this day? Would you believe me if I told you that they went on to open a business that they called C4 (Christian Couples Counseling Centers). What if I told you that they are now happier and stronger than they have ever been? More importantly, do you believe that *your* marriage can also be stronger and happier after enduring betrayal and infidelity?

You see, Kenneth and Lacey's marriage was tested by fire but they were not consumed. They learned and grew from their experience and have since dedicated their lives to helping couples overcome the same issues they did. They first did the necessary work to repair their own marriage. They made a commitment to pray together daily, go to counseling and to never allow a third party to enter their marriage again. It was not easy. At times, they both thought that it would be much easier to give up and get a divorce. They were right, divorce was the easier option but for them it was not the best option. If you asked them today, they would tell you that they are so glad that they decided to work it out and stay married. They have taken the time and care to build their safe house.

You've read Kenneth and Lacey's story but now it's time to tell your story. Using the lined pages in this section, write a summary or description of your marriage. You can write as little or as much as you like but be sure to capture all of the important milestones within your marriage. Next, take some time to take inventory of the people in your life. Write a one to two sentence summary about each person you call your friend. Include family members as well if applicable. Do any of their words or behaviors remind you of Shawndra? Is there anyone in your life that you have unsettling feelings about? Maybe someone who causes you to be unsure of their motives? If so, remember that those feelings are valid and should not be taken lightly. Be sure to remove those people from your life immediately. In this chapter, you will find a step by step guide to building your safe house. A major part of that process is ridding your life of any potential threats and dangers to your marriage.

Step 1: Address any suspicions or behaviors within your marriage that make you feel uncomfortable.

The best way to do this is to have an abundance of open and honest communication with your partner. In your conversations with your spouse, be sure to use "I" statements. For example, say things like "I feel sad when you ignore me" as opposed to "You made me angry when ignored me." It is important to understand that your partner cannot "make" you do anything or feel a certain emotion. Your actions and emotions are your choices and you should not place the responsibility of your actions or emotions on your spouse. In setting this standard for communication with your spouse, you will ensure that neither you or your partner is hurt or offended. Also, each partner will feel heard and understood.

Communication with your partner is crucial to the success of your relationship. By now, you have probably realized that it is one of the biggest problems within marriages. Without communication, a healthy relationship cannot exist. Do not avoid talking about issues with your partner because it is uncomfortable. Pray that God give you the courage to speak up and say what you are feeling.

Exercise: Practice using "I" statements in the next conversation that you have with your spouse and encourage them to do the same. Every time you catch yourself saying something like "You made me do this" stop, retract and rephrase using an "I" statement.

Step 2: Carefully assess and examine the culture within your marriage.

Does the culture of your marriage leave gaping holes where the enemy can creep in? Let's take a moment to dissect the word 'culture.' Culture has several definitions which are listed here: 1) the beliefs, customs, arts, etc., of a particular society, group, place or time 2) a particular society that has its own beliefs, ways of life, art, etc. 3) defined a way of thinking, behaving or working that exists in a place or organization. What can be said about the way of thinking, behaving and working that exists within your marriage? Write down some of the things that come to mind when thinking about the current culture of your marriage in the lined pages of this book.

In relation to Kenneth and Lacey's story, it is important to point out that infidelity is not about sex. It is about unmet emotional needs. This is why it is critical for both partners to possess high self-awareness. According to renowned licensed mental therapist Vladimire Calixte, being self-aware changes the way you live and the way you love. In many cases one or both parties in a marriage place the responsibility of maintaining their own emotional well-being on their partner or in Kenneth and Lacey's case, in a third party. Tasking your partner with maintaining your emotional well-being is setting them up for failure. In order to have a happy healthy marriage, you have to learn to take responsibility for your own emotional well-being.

Remember that being happy or unhappy is a choice and the choice is yours to make!

Exercise: Make a list of your emotional needs. Ask yourself the following questions: am I honest with myself about my feelings? What do I need to make me feel whole? What am I holding on to from my past? What do I need to forgive myself for? You will be surprised at how many things you will learn about yourself just by answering these questions. By having this type of conversation with yourself on a regular basis, you will unlock the door to meeting your emotional needs.

Step 3: Leave fourth, fifth and sixth parties out!

Your marriage is between you, God, and your mate. Period. There is no room for others. If there has been infidelity, the offending partner must cut off all contact with the person they were unfaithful with in order for a full reconciliation to happen. If there is a friend or family member who you have told about your marital problems, stop now. Do not tell them anything else. Family members will always take sides and friends don't need to know personal details about things that go on between you and your mate.

Step 4: Practice making daily deposits into your marriage

Here are a few ideas for finding ways to positively interact with your spouse each and every day:

1) Positive Flooding. Anytime you find your spouse doing something that warms your heart, praise them. It could be something as simple as cooking dinner for you or completing a household task that you normally do. No matter how minor the task, let your spouse know that you appreciate it. It is always a good idea to encourage behavior that you want your spouse to continue. Focus on what they are doing right instead of pointing out what they are doing wrong.

47

2) Be of service. Start the day by asking them "what do you need from me today?" Or "what can I say or do to make your day better?" This is such a simple way to make a positive impact on your partner. You will find that offering to improve their mood will improve your mood as well. This behavior in a marriage often becomes contagious. Do not be surprised when your partner reciprocates.

3) Be vulnerable. Let your partner really see you. Do not mask anything and do not pretend to be strong when you are not. There is power in vulnerability as it allows for a deeper connection between you and your mate.

4) Date your spouse. Do the things that you did to impress them before you got married. So many couples forget this step but it is a vital part of keeping your marriage fresh and exciting!

5) Speak each other's love language. *The 5 Love Languages* by Gary Chapman is a must read for couples. In it you will learn what the five love languages are and most importantly, which love language you primarily identify with. This is a direct way to positively impact the culture within your marriage on a daily basis. By actively and consistently speaking each other's love languages, you will see a dramatic improvement your daily interactions with your mate.

Step 5: Don't be afraid to seek professional help

There is often a negative connotation associated with going to counseling. This should not be the case! Regular visits to a licensed therapist is one of the best decisions you and your spouse can make. Society has placed a shameful cloud on asking for help, often mistaking needing help for weakness. Do not allow that cloud to hover over your life or your marriage! Also, know that asking for help is the exact opposite of weakness. It takes a great deal of strength and courage to admit that you need help and to proactively take those steps. Mental health professionals are trained to help you work through things that you may not be able to sort out on your own. Many people benefit from seeing a therapist on their own and along with their spouse.

Step 6: Actively invite God into your marriage

I saved the most important tip for last because I want it to have the most impact. When is the last time you prayed for your spouse, with your spouse? If you cannot remember, that needs to change today. When we invite God into our marriage on a daily basis, we are making a decision to let him work wonders in us and through us. Have you ever noticed that when you try to do something without God's input, it completely falls apart? However, when God is involved, things flow and come together perfectly. Your marriage is no different. Do not make the mistake of thinking that you do not need God to enter your marriage.

In my final thoughts, I want to let you know that I am in prayer for you. I am in prayer for your life and your marriage. I am in prayer for your loved ones, your finances, your career, your health, and the condition of your spirit. I pray that you walk in forgiveness, love, and light in spite of what you have experienced.

I pray that you use what you have been through to usher you to a breakthrough! I pray that you find reminders of God's love for you each and every day. I pray that you accept and embrace God's peace and do away with fear and worry. I pray that this book has blessed you in a mighty way.

I pray that reading it has changed the trajectory of your life for the better. I pray that this divine appointment has positively impacted your perspective on your marriage and your spouse.

I pray that you feel a shift in the atmosphere of your home every time you open this book! I pray that you bless someone in your life with this book after you have read it, because someone else that you know needs to read this too.

It is my hope that you feel empowered and able to apply the lessons laid out in the story of Kenneth and Lacey. I challenge you to believe God's promises for your life. I encourage you to walk in those promises daily! I pray that you always remember that our greatest tests in life are setting us up for our greatest testimonies.

Psalm 30:5 says "weeping may endure for a night, but joy comes in the morning."

You may very well be in the midst of your night season at this time; but if you just hold on to God's unwavering hand, you will surely see the morning come to pass in your situation. Not only will you see the morning, you will bask in the beauty of God's vision for your life as you are tucked soundly away in your Safe House.

Journal Page

_____

_____

_____

_____

_____

_____

_____

_____

_____

_____

About the Author

Highly sought after motivational speaker and coach, Cheryl A. Polote-Williamson is a two-time best-selling author. Her works include *Soul Reborn: A Book of Words, Motivations, and Inspirations*, and *Words from the Spirit for the Spirit*. Cheryl is also a coauthor of *Shift On* by Nikki Woods which features twenty stories of turning trials into triumph. Cheryl's first book was released in May 2013 and has inspired both men and women to not only pursue, but LIVE their dreams.

Cheryl holds a Bachelor of Science Degree in Criminal Justice from Shaw University. She is a member of Alpha Kappa Alpha Sorority, Inc., The Links, Inc., and the Christian Women in Media Association.

Deemed a savvy business woman after having owned Boxing Club Franchises within North and Central Texas and as partner of 924 Sports Management, LLC., Cheryl has been nationally recognized for her client relationships, entrepreneurial skills, and strategic partnerships.

As a Lover of GOD, Kingdompreneur, and member of St. John Church Unleashed, Cheryl places a deep emphasis on the importance of both business and personal relationships being solidly built on honesty, integrity, and trust. She addresses these topics in her blog series in which she tells of her own experiences of hurt and betrayal.

She consistently speaks on transformation, strength and wisdom through hosting her Soul Talk Radio Show and has previously been featured on Dallas Fox 4 News, Heaven 97 {970 AM Radio}, Denton Record Chronicle, as well as Rolling Out and Eclipse Magazines.

Philanthropists and pillars in their community, Cheryl and her Husband Russell have been married for 24 years and have three beautiful children, Russell Jr., Lauren, Courtney, along with an adorable granddaughter, Leah.

Contact Cheryl for speaking engagements, conferences, and book signings.

CPW
6101 Long Prairie Road
Suite 744 #269
Flower Mound, Texas
75028
Cherylpolote-Williamson.com
Cheryl Polote Williamson on Facebook
Author@cherylpolote-Williamson.com